# CREATION
# SINGS

# CREATION SINGS

## HOW GOD'S WORK DECLARES GOD'S TRUTH

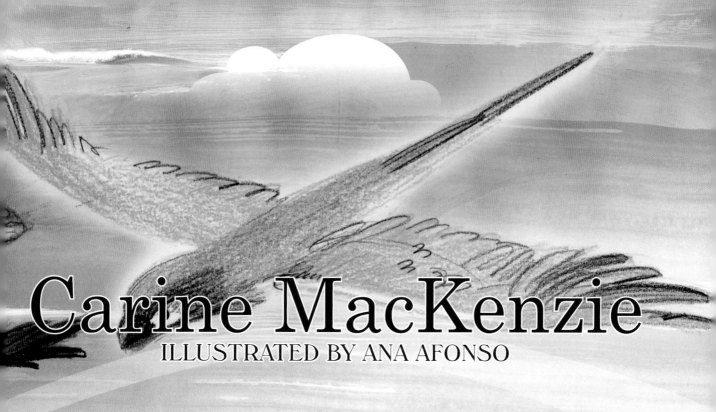

# Carine MacKenzie
## ILLUSTRATED BY ANA AFONSO

10 9 8 7 6 5 4 3 2 1
© Copyright 2016 Carine Mackenzie
ISBN:978-1-78191-785-5
Published by
Christian Focus Publications,
Geanies House, Fearn, Tain, Ross-shire, IV20 1TW, U.K.
Illustrations by Ana Afonso
Cover design by Daniel van Straaten
Printed in China

Written with love for my grandchildren:
Lydia, Esther, Philip,
Lois, Jack, Marianne, Isobel and Elizabeth
Ecclesiastes 12:1
CARINE MACKENZIE

# CONTENTS

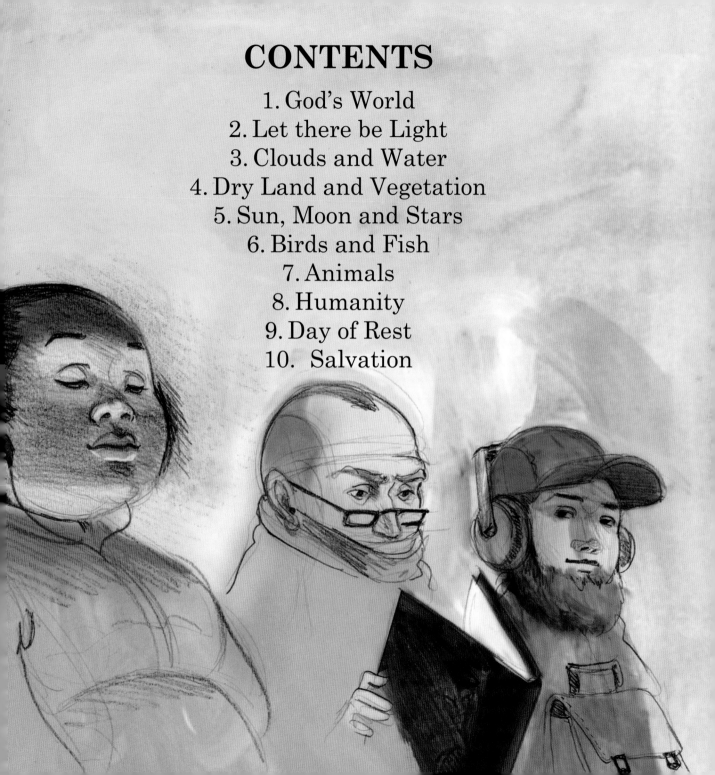

# 1. God's World

Our wonderful planet did not come into being by accident. God made the world from nothing. When we make a cake we use ingredients like flour and sugar. When we make a picture, we use paper and paints or crayons. But God created the world from nothing.

God is a Spirit. He has always existed. He is from everlasting to everlasting, with no beginning or end. We can never fully understand this. Our minds are too little to grasp the wonder of the all-powerful God. But we can believe what we learn of him in the Bible and worship him.

The Bible tells us that it is 'by faith we understand that the universe was created by the word of God, so that what is seen was not made out of things that are visible.' (Hebrews 11:3). By believing God, we know that the world was made at God's command; all made from nothing.

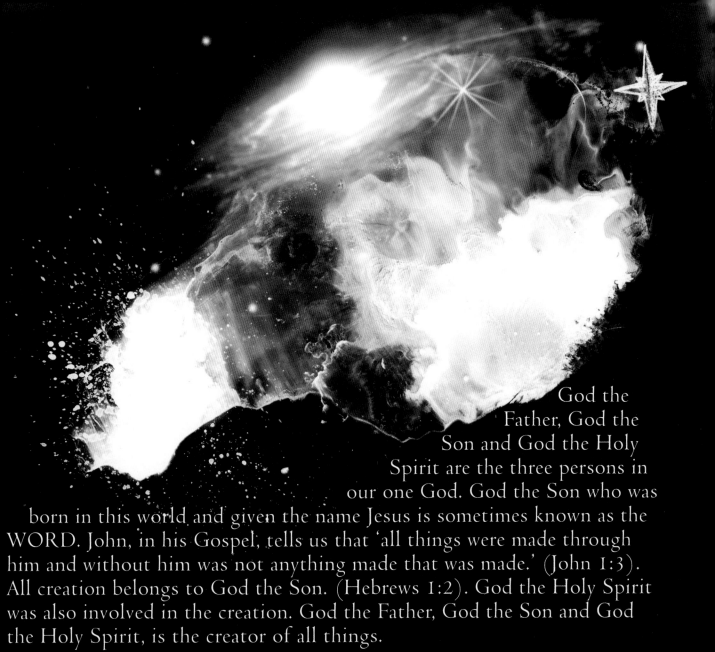

God the
Father, God the
Son and God the Holy
Spirit are the three persons in
our one God. God the Son who was
born in this world and given the name Jesus is sometimes known as the
WORD. John, in his Gospel, tells us that 'all things were made through
him and without him was not anything made that was made.' (John 1:3).
All creation belongs to God the Son. (Hebrews 1:2). God the Holy Spirit
was also involved in the creation. God the Father, God the Son and God
the Holy Spirit, is the creator of all things.

# Creation Sings

Before the mountains were brought forth, or ever you had formed the earth and the world, from everlasting to everlasting you are God. (Psalm 90:2).

# 2. Let there be Light

## Genesis 1: 1-9

On the first day, God created Light. He said, 'Let there be light' and light appeared immediately. God was pleased with the light that he had made. God separated the light from the darkness. God called the light DAY and the darkness NIGHT.

## Exodus 10:21-29

Light is a wonderful gift to us from God. When God's people, the Israelites, were in slavery in Egypt, Moses, God's prophet tried again and again to persuade Pharaoh the ruler to let them go. Time after time Pharaoh refused and each time God sent a punishment to the land of Egypt. The ninth punishment that God sent was the plague of darkness.

There was pitch darkness over all the land of Egypt for three days. The Egyptian people had to stay at home. They could not even see the person beside them, it was so dark. How frightening that must have been. But all the people of Israel had light as usual.

God who made the light in the beginning gave his people light and left their enemies in darkness.

# John 8:12

Jesus told us that he is the Light of the world. 'Whoever follows me,' he said, 'will not walk in darkness, but will have the light of life.' John 8:12. This light is not like a torch or a light bulb, but it describes the power that Jesus has to enlighten our understanding about God.

When we suddenly understand something that we read in the Bible, it is because Jesus the Light has helped us to see it. This is a light which never goes out.

This light will save us from the darkness of a lost eternity and from the darkness of a life lived far from God. Spiritual darkness is even more frightening than physical darkness, but God has given his people a wonderful solution, through his Son, Jesus Christ. If anyone is walking in darkness, with no light, 'let him trust in the name of the LORD and rely on his God.' (Isaiah 50:10).

# Creation Sings

For it is you who light my lamp;
the LORD my God lightens my darkness.  (Psalm 18:28).

# 3. Clouds and Water

Genesis 1: 6-8

On the second day, God created the atmosphere. When we look up to the sky, we see different types of clouds – some dark and full of rain, others white and fluffy. Every cloud in the sky has been made by God.

God made the seas and the oceans. All the water that covers more than half of the earth's surface was made by God.

God divided the atmosphere above from the waters below on the second day. The Lord used his creation to teach his people. When King Ahab was ruler over the land of Israel, he was more evil than any of the kings who ruled before him. He worshipped the false god, Baal. God was angry with him.

But God's prophet, Elijah, spoke God's message to King Ahab and the people.

God told Elijah to warn King Ahab. 'There will be no rain or dew on the land for many years.' Ahab was angry with this bad news and time and again caused trouble for Elijah. But God took care of him, and gave him a great victory over the prophets of Baal.

Elijah knew that God would send rain soon and so ease the drought. He climbed to the top of Mount Carmel to wait for the rain. 'Go and look towards the sea,' he told his servant. 'I cannot see anything unusual,' was the reply.

Seven times Elijah repeated the order. The answer was the same until the seventh time. 'There is a little cloud coming out from the sea; it looks no bigger than a man's hand.'

'Go to King Ahab,' ordered Elijah, 'and tell him to set off for home before the rain stops him.'

Soon the sky was covered with dark clouds; the wind blew and heavy rain began to fall. The drought was over.

The Lord was with Elijah, strengthening him and encouraging him. Elijah's confidence was in God.

Throughout his life, the Lord Jesus, who was the Son of God, showed his power over creation. One day, he and his disciples set out to sail across the Sea of Galilee. Jesus fell asleep in the boat because he was tired.

Soon a great storm blew up. The waves lashed over the boat. The disciples were terrified. They woke Jesus up. 'Lord, save us!' they shouted. 'We are going to drown.' Jesus stood up in the boat and spoke to the wind and the waves. 'Peace, be still!'

The wind stopped blowing. The sea became calm. God's powerful word had made the sea. Jesus, the Son of God, used his powerful word to calm the sea.

# Creation Sings

The heavens declare the glory of God,
and the sky above proclaims his handiwork.

(Psalm 19:1).

# 4. Dry Land and Vegetation

## Genesis 1: 9-13

On the third day, God spoke again. 'Let the waters be gathered together into one place and let the dry land appear.' Mountains and plains and valleys were created by his power. God called the dry land Earth and he called the water Seas.

God spoke again. 'Let the land produce vegetation, all sorts of plants and trees – flowers, bushes, great trees – all producing seed so that the vegetation would reproduce and spread. God saw that everything he had made was good.'

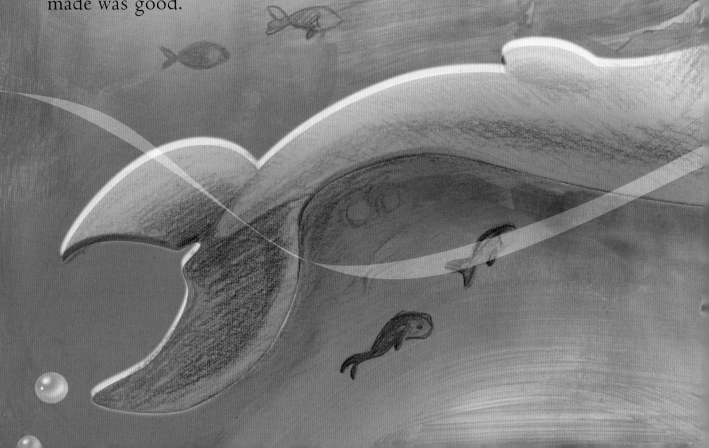

Jonah was reluctant to preach
God's message to the people of
Nineveh. In fact, he ran away to sea,
hoping to escape. But God had other plans.
A storm blew up, Jonah ended up in the sea; he was
swallowed by a great fish and vomited up again onto dry
land. What an adventure!

So Jonah eventually did preach in Nineveh. The people listened and repented of their sin and believed God.

Jonah ought to have been pleased, but instead he was angry, because God had not destroyed Nineveh as Jonah had said.

God taught Jonah a lesson. Jonah left the city in a bad mood. He climbed up to a place overlooking the city. He made a little shelter for himself and sat down to wait.

God, who has all the plants in his control, made a creeping plant, with big leaves, to grow up quickly. This gave very welcome shade to Jonah in the heat of the day.

God then sent a worm to gnaw at the roots so the plant died. The hot wind made Jonah more and more uncomfortable.

'You are sorry that the plant was destroyed,' said God. 'Should you not have had as much pity on that great city, Nineveh?'

Jonah had been shown great mercy himself in being spared from drowning. He should have rejoiced that God showed mercy to the thousands of people in Nineveh. The plant, the worm and the hot east wind, all made by God, were used to teach Jonah about God's mercy for his people.

Our loving God delights to show mercy to his people. He gives the wonderful gift of forgiveness of sin, because of the Lord Jesus Christ and what he has done on the cross to take the punishment on himself that is due to us for our sin. Christ died on the cross — made from the wood of a tree, a tree created by himself.

'He himself bore our sins in his body on the tree, that we might die to sin and live to righteousness.' (1 Peter 2:24)

# Creation Sings

He (the godly man) is like a tree,

planted by streams of water that yields its fruit in its season,

and its leaf does not wither.

In all that he does, he prospers.

(Psalm 1:3).

# 5. Sun, Moon and Stars

Genesis 1: 14-19

On the fourth day, God made the sun, the moon and the stars.
'Let there be lights in the skies,' he said. 'Let them bring order to the seasons and to the days and years; and let them be lights in the vast heavens.'

So God made the sun which shines on us during our day-time and the moon which we see shining in the sky at night. God also made the millions of stars which light up the night sky. God saw that what he had made was good.

Good King Hezekiah of Judah became very sick. The prophet Isaiah came to see him. 'Set your affairs in order and prepare to die,' he told him.

Hezekiah turned his face to the wall and wept. 'Oh, Lord,' he prayed, 'remember how I have always tried to obey you.'

Before Isaiah left the courtyard the Lord told him to go back to Hezekiah. 'Tell him that the Lord God has heard his prayer, and I will heal him. In three days he will be out of bed and at the temple. I will give him fifteen more years of life, and save him and the city from his enemy. This will be done for the glory of my own name and for the sake of my servant David.'

Isaiah told Hezekiah the good news, and told him to put a paste of dried figs on the infected boil.

'Show me a sign that the Lord will heal me,' Hezekiah asked Isaiah.

'The Lord will give you a sign. Do you want the shadow on the sun dial to go forward ten degrees or backward ten degrees?' replied Isaiah.

'The shadow always moves forward,' said Hezekiah. 'Make it go backwards ten degrees.'

Isaiah asked the Lord to do this and God graciously answered his prayer. God, who had made the sun, used it to reassure his servant, Hezekiah, of his love and care for him.

Wise men from the east noticed a strange star in the sky. 'This is a special star for the new born king of the Jews. We will go to worship him,' they said. When King Herod heard this, he was really worried. He called the chief priests and scribes to his palace in Jerusalem.

'Where will the Christ be born?' he asked.

The prophet Micah wrote that the ruler would come from Bethlehem in Judah.

Herod summoned the wise men and asked them when they first saw the star. 'Go and look for the child in Bethlehem and tell me when you find him,' he ordered.

The wise men went on their way and the star they had seen before went before them and came to rest above the place where the special baby, the Lord Jesus had been born.

When they saw the star they were very joyful. And when they saw the baby Jesus, they fell down and worshipped him.

God used one of the stars he had created to guide these men to the place where they could meet Jesus the Saviour of the world. God knows every star. He knows how many there are and he gives names to all of them. (Psalm 147:4)

Jesus is described as the bright morning star – the star shining in the early morning pointing to the coming daylight. (Revelation 22:16).

What does Jesus point us to? He points us to eternal life and salvation. He points us to God. He points us to a future that is free from sin when we trust in him and his sacrifice on the cross. But he does more than just point us to these things – he brings us there. He is God and brings us to God his heavenly Father.

The prophet Malachi described the Lord as the sun of righteousness bringing light and healing to those who fear the Lord.

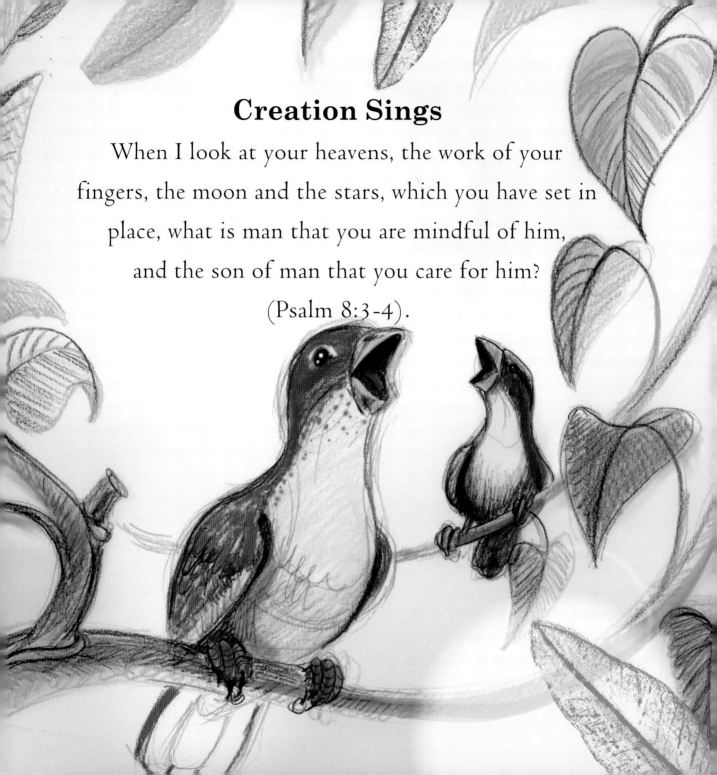

# Creation Sings

When I look at your heavens, the work of your fingers, the moon and the stars, which you have set in place, what is man that you are mindful of him, and the son of man that you care for him?

(Psalm 8:3-4).

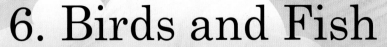

# 6. Birds and Fish

Genesis 1: 20-23

On the fifth day, God made the sea-creatures and birds. 'Let the waters be filled with living creatures,' God said, 'and let birds fly across the sky.'

With these words God made all sorts of sea creatures – the great shark and whale and the tiny shrimp and starfish and every kind of fish.

All the beautiful birds were made by God's word of power – the sparrow and the hawk, the graceful swan and the tiny wren.

God blessed all his creatures and gave them the ability to reproduce young. So the birds and the fish multiplied and filled the skies and the seas.

When there was drought in the land God told Elijah to go across the Jordan River and hide from angry King Ahab beside the brook Cherith. Elijah drank water from the brook and every morning and every evening ravens brought bread and meat for him to eat. God used the birds to take care of his servant Elijah.

In Capernaum, one day a man came up to Peter and asked, 'Does your master, Jesus, not pay temple tax?' 'Oh, yes,' Peter replied. In the house Jesus spoke to Peter about this. 'Would a king take tax money from his son or from others?' 'From others,' said Peter. 'Then the sons are free,' said Jesus who was the Son of God. 'But we do not want to give offence. Go to the sea, throw in a hook and take up the first fish you catch. When you open its mouth you will find a coin. That will be enough to pay the tax for us both.'

The fish was under the control of God who made it.

# Creation Sings

You (God) have given him (man)
dominion over the works of your hands
. . . the birds of the heaven
and the fish of the sea. (Psalm 8: 6-8)

# 7. Animals

Genesis 1: 24-25

On the sixth day, God made the animals. 'Let the earth produce living creatures,' said God. With these words all sorts of animals came into being – sheep and wolves and lions and mice and insects.

God saw that what he had made was good.

Daniel and his fellow countrymen, the Israelites, were taken captive to Babylon. In that foreign land, Daniel remained faithful to God. He prayed and worshipped God every day. He was promoted to a high position in the king's house. Other officials became jealous. They tried to find fault with Daniel, but he was honest and trustworthy in all his work.

'We will never catch Daniel out,' they said, 'unless we can think of something to do with his worshipping God.' So they hatched a plot. They persuaded the king to pass a law ordering everyone to pray only to him for thirty days. Anyone disobeying, would be thrown into a lions' den.

Daniel heard of this new law, but was determined to obey God rather than the king. He went immediately to pray to the Lord God as he always did three times a day. The jealous officials saw him by the open window and reported him to the king. Daniel was thrown into the lions' den. A big stone sealed the entrance. The next morning the king went nervously to the den to see what had happened to Daniel. He was delighted to hear Daniel's voice, 'My God sent his angel to shut the lions' mouths. They have not hurt me at all.'

God, who made the lions, shut the lions' mouths and kept Daniel safe.

God's creation is under his control all the time.

One day, Jesus asked his disciples if they knew who he was, 'You are the Christ,' Peter replied, 'the Son of the living God.' Jesus then warned his disciples that he would go to Jerusalem where he would suffer greatly and be killed. This was his great work of salvation for his people. He would rise from the dead on the third day.

So they headed for Jerusalem. When they came near to the Mount of Olives, Jesus called two of his disciples over. 'Go to that village over there,' he said. 'You will find a young donkey tethered. It has never been ridden before. Untie him and bring him to me. If anyone asks you what you are doing, tell them that the Lord needs this donkey.'

The humble donkey carried the King of kings, into the city of Jerusalem, where he died to pay the price of sin for his people who are from every tribe and tongue and nation.

# Creation Sings

The voice of the Lord makes the deer give birth and strips the forest bare, and in his temple all cry, "Glory!" Psalm 29:9.

# Creation Sings

Your righteousness is like the mighty mountains,
your justice like the great deep.
You, LORD, look after people and animals. Psalm 36:6.

# 8. Humanity
Genesis 1: 26-31, 2:18-25

Then God reached the climax of his creative work. 'Let us make man in our image,' God said, 'Man will rule over the fish and the birds and the animals' The Lord made a man from the dust of the ground. He breathed the breath of life into his nostrils and man became a living soul. The man was called Adam.

God did not want Adam to be alone so he made a woman to be his helper and companion. He caused Adam to fall into a deep sleep. While he was sleeping, God took one of Adam's ribs, then closed the flesh again. From this rib, God made a woman called Eve. Adam was very glad to have Eve as his wife. God blessed Adam and Eve, told them to have children and rule over all the other living creatures.

God has made all human beings in his own image. We are different from the animals. God has given us a soul. We have brains that can think logically and solve problems. We have a conscience and feel guilty when we do wrong. God has told us to be holy as he is holy, but we fall far short.

In the Bible we read of different people who showed many God-given qualities. Solomon was very wise; Moses was very meek; Abigail was clever and tactful; David was brave; Jonathan was loving and gracious; Job was blameless and upright, one who feared God and turned away from evil.

But there was only ever one man who lived a perfect life – one who was truly upright and wise and meek in all that he did. That man was the Lord Jesus Christ. God the Father was well pleased with Jesus. He lived the perfect life for us and died for us on the cross to save us from our sins.

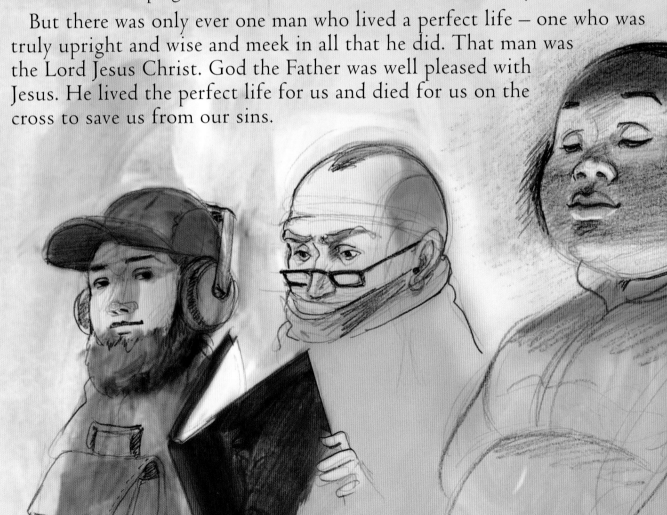

Jesus was the perfect man – perfect in wisdom, holiness and goodness. He was 'the truth' and always did and said what was true. He was powerful with authority over life and nature and disease and demons.

Jesus said, 'All authority in heaven and on earth has been given to me.' (Matthew 28:18).

# Creation Sings

Know that the Lord, he is God! It is he who made us, and we are his; we are his people, and the sheep of his pasture. (Psalm 100:3)

# 9. Day of Rest

## Genesis 2:1-3

God's great work of creation was completed. On the seventh day, he rested. He was not tired or weary but wanted to show that his work of creation was done. God blessed this day and made it holy. He gave it to us for our benefit and blessing, for our body, mind and soul. Jesus told us 'the Sabbath was made for man, not man for the Sabbath.' (Mark 2:27). This is one day every week when we remember God in a special way and worship him with his people.

Moses led the children of Israel from Egypt to the Promised Land. God took care of them in spite of their rebellion and complaints. On the journey, God gave special instructions which are for us too. They are called the Ten Commandments. One of these tells us to remember the Sabbath day to keep it holy.

God graciously provided food for his people as they travelled through the wilderness. Each morning the ground was covered with little white seeds called manna. Each family collected what they needed for the day. On the sixth day of the week they collected twice as much, some to eat on the Sabbath day. God did not send manna on the Sabbath.

It was Jesus' custom to go the synagogue to worship on the Sabbath. He kept the law of God perfectly and always kept the Sabbath, although some men found fault when he healed the sick on the Sabbath. Jesus assured them that it was lawful to do good on the Sabbath.

The Christian Sabbath is on the first day of the week, Sunday, the day on which the Saviour rose from the grave.

Christians meet together to worship God and have fellowship together. When Paul and his fellow travellers reached Philippi, they met with a group of women at the riverside. They had met to pray together. Paul preached to them. Lydia, who knew about God's Word, heard Paul's message. On that day, her heart was opened to respond quietly to the Lord Jesus. She became a true believer.

# Creation Sings

This is the day that the LORD has made;

let us rejoice and be glad in it.

(Psalm 118:24)

# 10. Salvation

Genesis 3: 1-24

God's creation was perfect. Adam and Eve were perfect. But soon sin entered the world. Satan, in the form of a serpent, tempted Eve to disobey God. God had told Adam and Eve not to eat fruit from one particular tree. But Eve listened to Satan's lies and she took some of the fruit and gave some to Adam. Adam and Eve were no longer perfect. The world was no longer perfect.

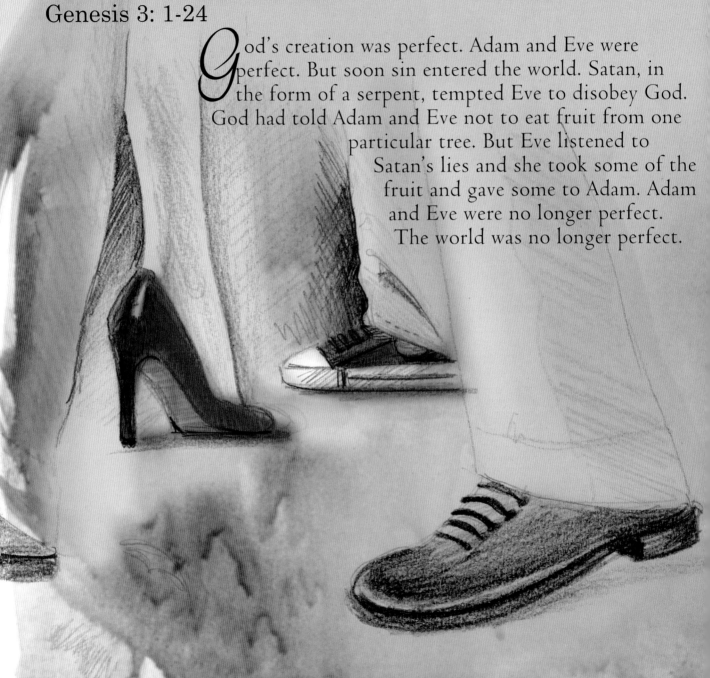

Our world now has ugliness and pollution and disease.

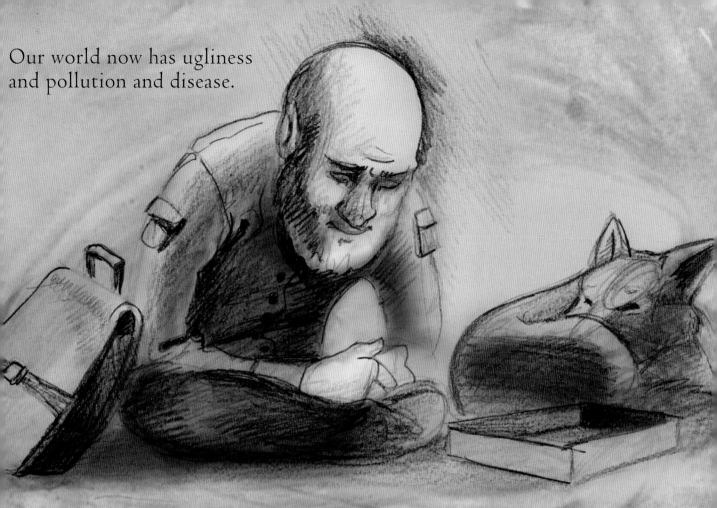

People are greedy and cruel and untruthful. God is holy and just. He hates sin and has to punish it. Adam and Eve were put out of the beautiful garden. They then lived lives of pain and toil and sorrow. Death became a reality to face.

However, God still showed mercy to Adam and Eve, and to their children and to us. God spoke to the serpent and told him there would be enmity between him and the woman, between his offspring and hers. 'The woman's Son will crush your head and you will hurt his heel.'

This was the first hint of the coming Saviour. The Lord Jesus Christ, the Son of God and the offspring of a woman would be bruised and wounded on the cross as he died for sinners, but in doing that he would defeat death and crush Satan, the evil one.

Jesus, the Creator, fulfilled all God's promises. He came to earth as a human like us: he lived a perfect life which we cannot do; he died to pay the price for sin; he was buried but conquered death and sin; he rose from the dead and then ascended into heaven, where he reigns as a Prince and a Saviour, reigning over his creation.

God tells us in the Bible that the world as we know it will be destroyed one day. The elements will be destroyed by fire and the earth laid bare.

God urges us to live holy and godly lives. Those who trust in the Lord Jesus will be safe. God has promised a new heaven and a new earth, the home of righteousness. (2 Peter 3:11-13).

The same power which made the world will make a new one. With God all things are possible. To God be the glory!

God's love will never end. God's Word will never end. It is from everlasting to everlasting.

## Creation Sings

For God so loved the world that he gave
his only Son, that whoever believes in
him should not perish but have eternal life. (John 3:16)

# Christian Focus Publications

Christian Focus Publications publishes books for adults and children under its four main imprints: Christian Focus, CF4K, Mentor and Christian Heritage. Our books reflect our conviction that God's Word is reliable and Jesus is the way to know him, and live for ever with him. Our children's list includes a Sunday School curriculum that covers pre-school to early teens, and puzzle and activity books. We also publish personal and family devotional titles, biographies and inspirational stories that children will love. If you are looking for quality Bible teaching for children, then we have an excellent range of Bible stories and age-specific theological books. From pre-school board books to teenage apologetics, we have it covered!

CF4•K